FOSSILS

BY SALLY M. WALKER

LERNER PUBLICATIONS COMPANY • MINNEAPOLIS

Library of Congress Cataloging-in-Publication Data

Walker, Sally M.
    Fossils / by Sally M. Walker.
    p.   cm. — (Early bird earth science)
    Includes index.
    ISBN-13: 978–0–8225–5945–0 (lib. bdg. : alk. paper)
    ISBN-10: 0–8225–5945–5 (lib. bdg. : alk. paper)
    1. Fossils—Juvenile literature. 2. Paleontology—Juvenile literature. I. Title. II. Series.
    QE714.5.W345 2007
    560—dc22   2005023728

Manufactured in the United States of America
1 2 3 4 5 6 – JR – 12 11 10 09 08 07

CONTENTS

BE A WORD DETECTIVE

Can you find these words as you read about fossils? Be a detective and try to figure out what they mean. You can turn to the glossary on page 46 for help.

ancient	minerals	sedimentary
asphalt	molds	rock
cast	paleontologist	sediments
coquina	preserved	
fossils	remains	

These are the remains of an animal that lived long ago. What are remains?

CHAPTER 1

WHAT IS A FOSSIL?

Fossils are the hardened remains of plants and animals. Remains are parts left behind after plants or animals die. All fossils are old. Fossils are the traces and remains of plants and animals that lived more than 10,000 years ago.

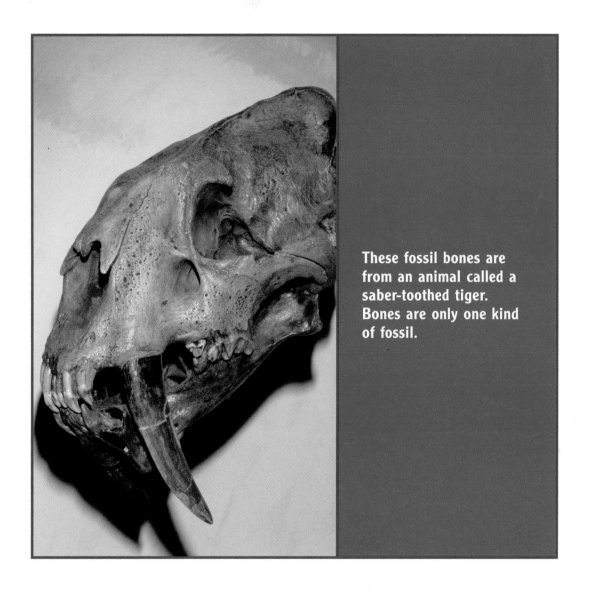

These fossil bones are from an animal called a saber-toothed tiger. Bones are only one kind of fossil.

There are many different kinds of fossils. Dinosaur bones are fossils. Dinosaur teeth are fossils too. Claws, eggs, and nests can be fossils. So can leaves, flower petals, and plant stems.

Shells from ancient (AYN-shuhnt) clams and snails are fossils. *Ancient* means "very old." The body parts of insects also can become fossils. Have you ever seen an insect that has turned into a fossil?

Clams are animals with hard shells. They live underwater.

A dinosaur made this ancient footprint.

Ancient footprints are another kind of fossil. Scientists have found many ancient footprints. Some of the footprints are from human beings. Others are from dinosaurs.

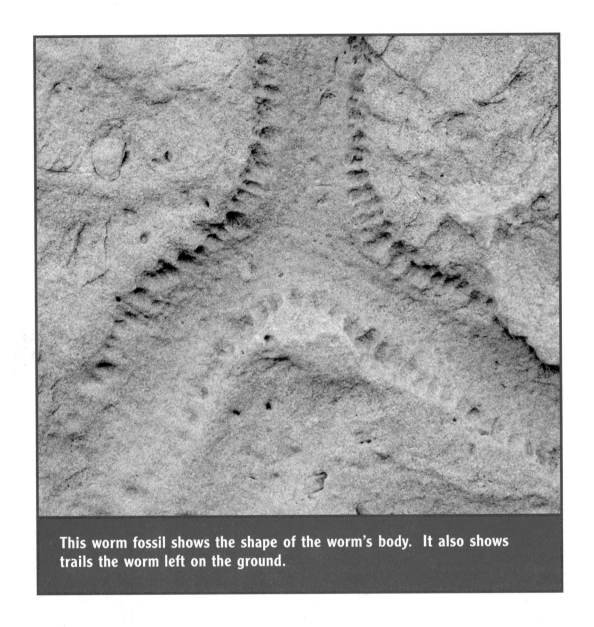

This worm fossil shows the shape of the worm's body. It also shows trails the worm left on the ground.

Animal trails can be fossils. Snails and worms make trails in mud. These trails show where an animal went.

10

Bones, tracks, and trails are all signs of life from long ago. And all of them can become fossils. But how do flower petals or dinosaur bones turn into fossils?

Leaf fossils are signs of plants that lived long ago.

This tooth became a fossil. What happens to most plant and animal remains?

CHAPTER 2

HOW DO FOSSILS FORM?

Fossils are plant and animal remains that have been naturally preserved. That means that they were saved without help from people. Most remains disappear over time. Other animals eat them or carry them away. Uneaten remains slowly rot. They become soft and fall apart.

Rock often surrounds dinosaur bones. Rock protects the bones.

But sometimes, remains get buried. Then the remains are protected. They do not rot as quickly as remains that are not protected. They are hidden from animals that might eat them. The remains are also safe from water and wind. Water and wind can scatter remains. They can break remains apart.

Ice can preserve remains. If ice covers the body of an animal that has died, the frozen body can last for many years. At one time, ice covered much of Earth. Many frozen plants and animals became fossils then.

Buried bones can last for a very long time. These buried dinosaur bones were discovered in China.

This is a fossil hair from an animal called a woolly mammoth. Hair is a soft body part.

Ice preserves plants and animals very well. It can even preserve an animal's soft body parts, such as fur, skin, and muscles. Soft body parts don't usually become fossils. Most soft body parts rot quickly. So scientists are excited when they find fur, skin, or muscle fossils.

Tar pits can preserve remains. Tar pits are pools full of asphalt (AS-fahlt). Asphalt is black and sticky. It comes from inside Earth. Sometimes animals fall into the asphalt. Then they get stuck. After a while, they die.

This pool of asphalt is at the La Brea Tar Pits. The La Brea Tar Pits are in Los Angeles, California. The animals are statues of creatures that lived long ago.

This saber-toothed tiger fossil was found at the La Brea Tar Pits.

When an animal dies in a tar pit, most of its body rots. But its teeth and bones do not rot. The asphalt preserves these hard body parts. When scientists dig in tar pits, they often find the teeth and bones of animals that lived long ago.

Millions of sediments piled up to make these layers.

Sediments (SEH-duh-mehnts) can preserve remains. Sediments are bits of mud, sand, stone, shell, or bone. Sediments cover plant and animal remains like a blanket. Most fossils are remains that were buried by sediments.

A blanket of sediments is called a layer. Some sediment layers are thin. Some sediment layers are thick. Layers can stack up on top of one another. Stacked sediment layers can be thousands of feet deep. Sediment layers can form on land or under water.

This is Fossil Butte National Monument. It is in Wyoming. Can you see the sediment layers? Many people look for fossils in the layers.

A deep stack of sediment layers is very heavy. The weight pushes the sediments together. Over time, chemicals (KEHM-uh-kuhlz) in the sediments make them stick together. Then the sediments harden into rock. Rock that is made in this way is called sedimentary (SEH-duh-MEHN-tuh-ree) rock. Fossils are often found in sedimentary rock.

Fossils are inside this sedimentary rock.

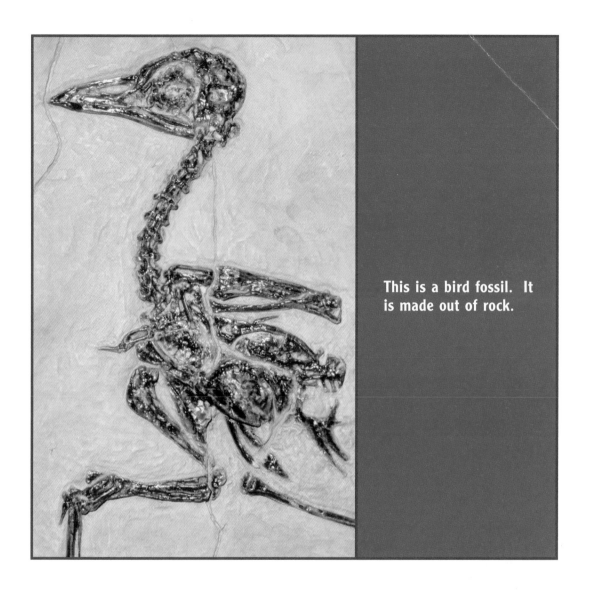

This is a bird fossil. It is made out of rock.

If remains are inside layers of sediments, they turn into rock along with the sediments. When plant or animal remains turn into rock, they become fossils.

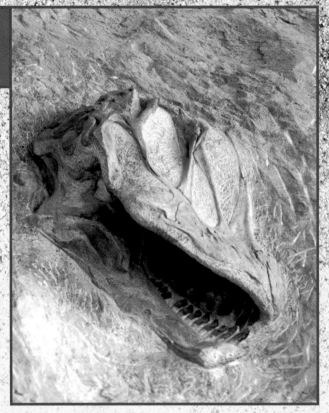

Groundwater often seeps into buried bones. What is groundwater?

CHAPTER 3

DO BONES REALLY TURN INTO STONE?

All bones have tiny holes in them. Sometimes groundwater soaks into the holes. Groundwater is water that is under the ground.

Rocks are made of minerals.

Groundwater has dissolved chemicals in it. The chemicals join together inside the bones. When the chemicals join together, they form minerals (MIHN-ur-uhlz). Minerals are the ingredients that make up rocks.

The minerals fill a bone's holes. The minerals become hard. They make the bone hard too. They also make the bone heavy. Sometimes the bone dissolves over time. But the minerals do not dissolve. They stay in the same place. They preserve the bone's shape. They become a fossil.

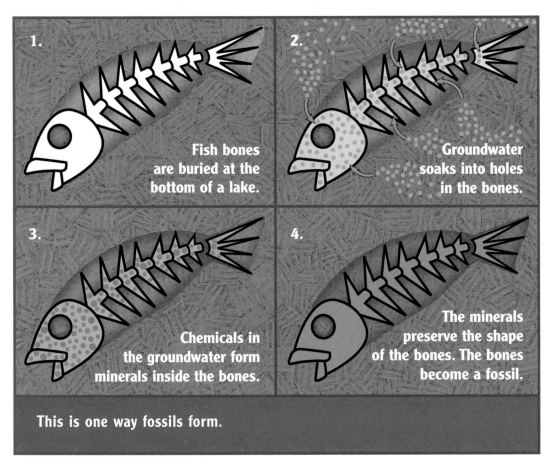

1. Fish bones are buried at the bottom of a lake.

2. Groundwater soaks into holes in the bones.

3. Chemicals in the groundwater form minerals inside the bones.

4. The minerals preserve the shape of the bones. The bones become a fossil.

This is one way fossils form.

Minerals turned these tree trunks into fossils.

A piece of wood has tiny spaces in it too. Water full of dissolved chemicals can soak into the spaces. The chemicals may become minerals. If the minerals form in the spaces, then the wood becomes a fossil.

Shell fossils are often molds. Molds are hollow spaces. Molds form after sediments bury plant or animal remains. Over time, the sediments turn into rock. Chemicals dissolve the remains. Then a hollow space is left behind. The mold shows the exact shape of the remains.

These are fossil snail shells. The arrow is pointing to a mold.

Sometimes water and chemicals fill the hollow space. Minerals form inside the mold. When they do, they make another kind of fossil. A fossil that formed inside a mold is called a cast.

The fossil on the left is a mold. The fossil on the right is a cast.

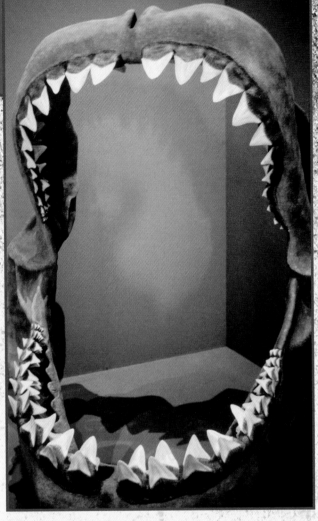

Fossil shark teeth are easy to find. But some fossils are hard to find. Why are some fossils hard to find?

CHAPTER 4
FINDING FOSSILS

Fossils are found in many places. Some fossils are easy to find. People often find fossil shark teeth on beaches near the ocean.

Sometimes fossils are hidden deep inside a rock. These fossils were hidden inside sedimentary rock.

Other fossils are hard to find. Many fossils are hidden inside sedimentary rock. Scientists must dig through the rock to find them.

A scientist who collects and studies fossils is called a paleontologist (PAY-lee-uhn-TAHL-uh-jihst). Paleontologists study many kinds of fossils.

Fossils can be big or small. Some fossils are so small that paleontologists need microscopes to see them. Microscopes are tools that make small things look big.

Some rocks have many fossils in them. The smallest fossils are very hard to see.

Big fossils, such as these shark teeth, are easy to see.

Bigger fossils are often mixed with soil. Paleontologists sift the soil through a screen. This helps them uncover the fossils. The soil passes through the holes, but the fossils do not.

Very large fossils such as shark teeth are easy to see. Paleontologists just pick them up.

Fossils are often buried in rocks. This rock is on the Kaibab Plateau. The plateau has many fossils.

Sometimes a fossil is hidden inside a piece of rock. Then a paleontologist uses a special hammer to chip away the rock.

Some fossils are too heavy to lift. A large fossil may also be fragile (FRAJ-uhl). That means that it breaks easily. Paleontologists must be careful not to break fragile fossils while they are moving them.

Some large fossils break easily.

Paleontologists wrap fragile fossils to protect them. The paleontologists wet strips of cloth in a mixture of water and plaster. Plaster is a white material that gets hard as it dries. Paleontologists cover the fossil with the wet cloth strips. When the cloth strips dry, they become a hard plaster shell. The shell protects the fossil.

A paleontologist peels away the plaster shell that is protecting a fossil.

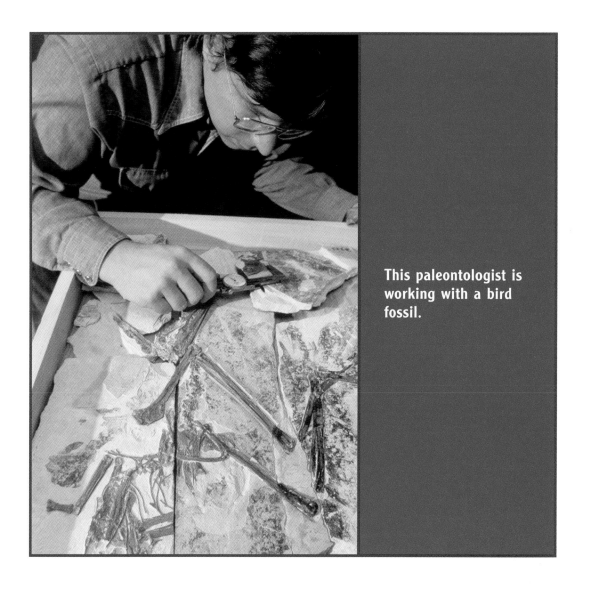

This paleontologist is working with a bird fossil.

When fossils are protected by hard plaster shells, paleontologists can move them. They can safely carry the fossils to places where they can study them.

Paleontologists study leaf fossils such as this one. What can paleontologists learn by studying fossils?

CHAPTER 5

WHY DO WE STUDY FOSSILS?

Paleontologists study fossils because they are important clues. Fossils can help paleontologists learn about ancient plants and animals.

36

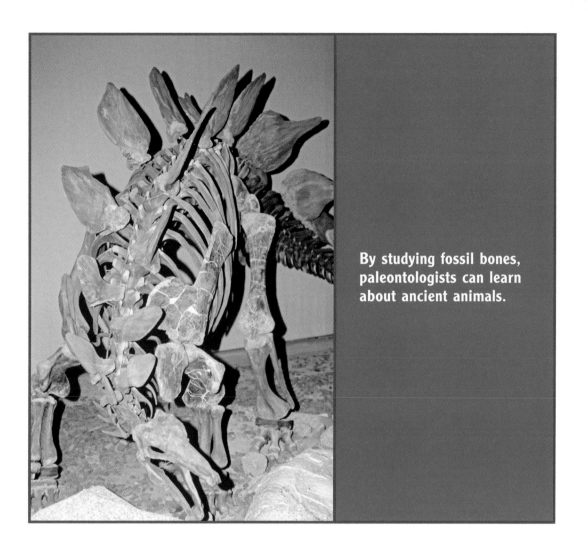

By studying fossil bones, paleontologists can learn about ancient animals.

Fossil bones can tell paleontologists what an animal may have looked like. The paleontologists can figure out how big an animal was. They may be able to learn how the animal moved.

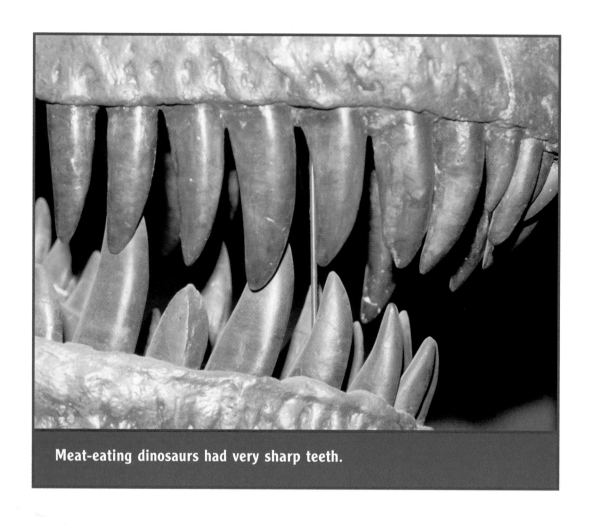

Meat-eating dinosaurs had very sharp teeth.

The shapes of fossil teeth tell paleontologists what kinds of foods an animal may have eaten. Animals that eat meat have sharp teeth. Sharp teeth can slice meat the way knives do. Animals that eat plants have flat teeth. Flat teeth can chew and grind leaves.

Fossils teach paleontologists about Earth's past. They give clues about what the weather and the land were like long ago. Some plants grow only in warm places. But sometimes fossils of those plants are found in a cold place. That tells us that at one time, the place was much warmer. Sometimes fish fossils are found in dry deserts. What do you think that means?

Sometimes fish fossils are found in dry areas. That tells us that water used to cover these areas.

Many sidewalks are made of concrete.

Paleontologists are not the only people who work with fossils. Did you know that you use fossils almost every day? Sidewalks and some buildings are made of concrete. Concrete is made of crushed sedimentary rocks. Crushed sedimentary rocks are filled with fossils.

Coquina (ko-KEE-nuh) is one type of sedimentary rock. Coquina is made of shell fossils. Blocks of coquina are used to make houses and walls.

Coquina blocks are made of shells like these.

Have you ever written with chalk? Chalk is made of fossils too. The fossils that become chalk once lived in the sea. These fossils are very small. You would need a microscope to see them.

Chalk is made out of fossils.

Many science museums have fossils you can see.

Fossils tell part of Earth's story. Studying fossils is a fun way to learn about the past. Do you have a favorite fossil? What kind of story does it tell you?

A NOTE TO ADULTS
ON SHARING A BOOK

When you share a book with a child, you show that reading is important. To get the most out of the experience, read in a comfortable, quiet place. Turn off the television and limit other distractions, such as telephone calls. Be prepared to start slowly. Take turns reading parts of this book. Stop occasionally and discuss what you're reading. Talk about the photographs. If the child begins to lose interest, stop reading. When you pick up the book again, revisit the parts you have already read.

BE A VOCABULARY DETECTIVE

The word list on page 5 contains words that are important in understanding the topic of this book. Be word detectives and search for the words as you read the book together. Talk about what the words mean and how they are used in the sentence. Do any of these words have more than one meaning? You will find the words defined in a glossary on page 46.

WHAT ABOUT QUESTIONS?

Use questions to make sure the child understands the information in this book. Here are some suggestions:

What did this paragraph tell us? What does this picture show? What do you think we'll learn about next? What is a fossil? How do fossils form? What are sediments? What do you call a scientist who studies fossils? How do we use fossils? What is your favorite part of this book? Why?

If the child has questions, don't hesitate to respond with questions of your own, such as What do *you* think? Why? What is it that you don't know? If the child can't remember certain facts, turn to the index.

INTRODUCING THE INDEX

The index helps readers find information without searching through the whole book. Turn to the index on page 48. Choose an entry such as *tar pits* and ask the child to find out why there are so many fossils in tar pits. Repeat with as many entries as you like. Ask the child to point out the differences between an index and a glossary. (The index helps readers find information, while the glossary tells readers what words mean.)

LEARN MORE ABOUT
FOSSILS

BOOKS

Larson, Peter, and Kristin Donnan. *Bones Rock! Everything You Need to Know to Be a Paleontologist.* Montpelier, VT: Invisible Cities Press, 2004. This book discusses fossil hunting and explains what it's like to work as a paleontologist.

Walker, Sally M. *Mystery Fish: Secrets of the Coelacanth.* Minneapolis: Millbrook Press, 2006. Learn all about an ancient fish called the coelacanth.

Williams, Judith. *Discovering Dinosaurs with a Fossil Hunter.* Berkeley Heights, NJ: Enslow Publishers, 2004. Read more about paleontologists and the fossils they study.

Zimmerman, Howard. *Dinosaurs!: The Biggest, Baddest, Strangest, Fastest.* New York: Atheneum Books for Young Readers, 2000. This fun book looks at many different kinds of dinosaurs.

WEBSITES

Page Museum at the La Brea Tar Pits
http://www.tarpits.org
This site has information about the Page Museum, which is located at the famous La Brea Tar Pits in Los Angeles, California.

San Diego Natural History Museum: Dinosaur Dig
http://www.sdnhm.org/kids/dinosaur
This page from the San Diego Natural History Museum includes fun information on fossils, dinosaurs, reptiles, and more.

Science News for Kids
http://www.sciencenewsforkids.org
This site offers articles on dinosaurs and fossils, animals, the environment, and more. It also has games, science fair news, and information on science experiments.

GLOSSARY

ancient (AYN-shuhnt): very old

asphalt (AS-fahlt): a sticky, black substance that comes from inside Earth. Asphalt is used to make roads.

cast: a fossil that forms inside a hollow space

coquina (ko-KEE-nuh): a kind of rock that is made of shell fossils

fossils: hardened parts left behind after plants or animals die. Tracks, trails, and molds also can be fossils.

minerals (MIHN-ur-uhlz): solid substances that are not alive. Rocks are made of minerals.

molds: hollow spaces that form after bits of mud, sand, stone, shell, or bone bury remains and the remains rot away

paleontologist (PAY-lee-uhn-TAHL-uh-jihst): a scientist who collects and studies fossils

preserved: saved from being destroyed

remains: parts left behind after plants or animals die

sedimentary (SEH-duh-MEHN-tuh-ree) rock: rock that forms when bits of mud, sand, stone, shell, or bone are squeezed together

sediments (SEH-duh-mehnts): bits of mud, sand, stone, shell, or bone

INDEX

Pages listed in **bold** type refer to photographs.

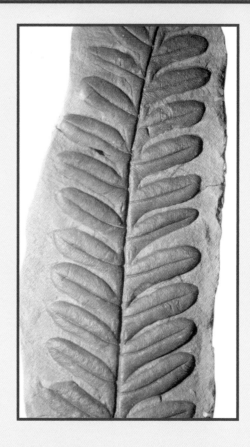